FROM LINDA
XMAS 2010

SOUTH SHIELDS

THROUGH TIME
Michael J. Hallowell

AMBERLEY PUBLISHING

First published 2008
Reprinted 2010

Amberley Publishing Plc
Cirencester Road, Chalford,
Stroud, Gloucestershire, GL6 8PE

www.amberley-books.com

British Library Cataloguing in Publication Data.
A catalogue record for this book is available from the British Library.

ISBN 978 1 84868 071 5

Typesetting and Origination by Amberley Publishing.
Printed in Great Britain.

For Robin and Louis,
and to the canny folks o' Shields from days gone by, who helped create
one of our nation's greatest towns.

Acknowledgements

South Tyneside Local Studies Library, including Hildred Whale, Ann Sharp and Keith Bardwell, for their unstinting assistance and advice, and for permission to reproduce many of the photographs in this volume, including those held at the library and a small number of others found in George B. Hodgson's book The Borough of South Shields.

Ivor Muncey, Caroline Sanderson, David Hutchinson, Jean Ward, Peter Hallowell and the late Evelyn Waugh-Almond for supplying some of the photographs used in this book and giving permission for their use.

Doreen Monteiro, for her kindness and encouragement, and for helping me access a number of photographs used in this book.

Credit should also be given in no small measure to several photographers who are no longer with us but whose snapshots from time are also included: J. Willits, Amy Flagg, R. Hodge, W. Parry, Ernest Fetch, Bob Watson and Jane Watson.

Sarah Flight, my editor at Amberley Publishing, for her tireless assistance and support.

Finally, thanks must also go to Peter Short, Ken Sutton, Ray Burchall and the many other correspondents who have contacted me since the first edition of this book was published, and to the eagle-eyed few who spotted the odd error here and there!

* * *

In assembling this collection of photographs I have rigorously attempted to detail, wherever possible, their origin and to credit the photographers and or/copyright holders. In a small number of cases it has proved impossible to ascertain these details. Should readers be able to supply me with any information regarding these images it will of course be included in future editions.

Introduction

I was born in South Shields, in the maternity ward of the General Hospital, and spent the first six years of my life there. My family and I lived in an upstairs flat in Armstrong Terrace, and, despite my tender years, I have vivid memories of my childhood. I recall going to Patterson's – or it may have been Pattison's – Dairy across the road to purchase milk, buying custard tarts at the bakery around the corner and, curiously, sitting in my high chair as a toddler eating a Farley's rusk. It's strange how incidental details like that stick in your mind. But then again, I've always believed that history is made up of incidental details. Professional historians may stand in awe at Glamis Castle, or pick over the events that led up to World War I, but to me real history concerns the way that life, and the passing of it, affects the day-to-day activities of the people. One old photograph can tell more than a thousand books when it comes to real history.

South Shields has a long and noble history stretching back over the centuries. It has played host to some of the finest shipbuilders in the world, the most skilled miners in the country and a veritable legion of renowned artists, writers and playwrights. South Shields has a lot to be proud of.

The borough has seen some tough times, most brought about by economic deprivation. It has known good times, too; Sand Dancers – to give Shields folk their collective colloquial epithet – have a natural enthusiasm and buoyancy that oft turns a bad situation into a good one. Their humour and self-deprecating wit is a true gift, and I can't think of another town I'd be prouder to call my birthplace.

In the early 1980s my wife and I lived in Taylor Street. Times were hard, and our weekly treat was a packet of chips and a bottle of Newcastle Brown Ale on a Friday night whilst sitting in front of the TV. We couldn't even afford carpets. If I could metaphorically rewind the tape and change things, would I? No; tough times forge people, make them stronger. Maybe that's what makes Shields folk special, for most have gone through tough times in one way or another.

The pictures in this book are a mixture of the civic and the personal, the public and the private. A small number you'll have seen before, whilst others are taken from private collections. One or two were even snapped with mobile phones. Some of the photographs in this book are quite beautiful, others historically enchanting. Some are a bit rough around the edges and would hardly win an award, but are included because they seemed to "capture the moment", so to speak. Collectively they display South Shields through the ages.

Today, the town has been "greened", and is a wonderful place for tourists to visit. It was not always so. Some of the photographs illustrate a stark contrast between the South Shields of today and the town of, say, 100 years ago. Each one tells a story, and as the years roll on, no doubt many more will be written.

Since the first edition of this book was published, a number of readers have contacted me and pointed out several minor errors, which have been corrected. I am indebted to them.

Mike Hallowell
May, 2010

South Shields is a riverside town, and the relationship between the town and the Tyne is strong. In past times the fishermen would take to the water in their small boats or "cobles". Here we can see the entrance to the old "Coble Landing" just off Shadwell Street. On the left is all that remains of the R. J. Marshall marine engineering works, a long-established family business which eventually ceased trading in 1884 when it was taken over by the Wapping Engine Works Company, Ltd. The paint is peeling and the doors and windows are all boarded, indicating the passage of a number of years between the closing down of the business and the taking of this photograph.

The new entrance to Coble Landing couldn't be more different. Swish new apartments grace the riverside, offering a far different environment to the one that R. J. Marshall knew. The grinding poverty has gone, and, inevitably, much of the area's character. That can't be helped, but there's no denying that, architecturally, Coble Landing is now a thing of beauty.

South Tyneside Libraries

Although much of Shadwell Street was tumbledown, Coble Landing itself was extremely picturesque. In this old picture we can see the Coble Inn, a small alehouse owned by J. P. Burke. It isn't known exactly when the Coble Inn was built, but the pub isn't mentioned on a list of the town's inns published in 1871.

The Coble Inn was later renamed "The Coble" and taken over by David Craig, whilst Thomas Hindmarsh opened a rival establishment with exactly the same name. Not to be outdone, one Mary Young followed suit which led to three pubs of the same name in the same street.

On the wooden gantry just in front of the pub a man and two youths, probably fishermen, can be seen chatting. Just in front of the gantry is an upturned coble, whilst to the right is a larger boat. Behind the coble are two carts, the smaller of which was probably used for transporting the cobles to the repair shops at Marshall's where several were in operation.

To the right of the Coble Inn is a building of older construction, the roof of which has began to sink. The large foundation stones may be the remains of an older quay, probably dating back to the eighteenth century.

Behind the new entrance to Coble Landing can be seen the Alum Ale House, one of the oldest drinking establishments in the town, parts of which date back to the early part of the eighteenth century.

Coble Landing was known as Ferry Landing for a while. Here we can see Marshall's Quay, and a young chap sitting on the step of one of the waterfront taverns. An upturned boat, possibly awaiting repair, lies outside of one of the repair shops on the quay.

The new Ferry Landing can be found to the west, only a short walk from the site of its original location. The contrast is stark; seasoned timber has been replaced with brightly-painted steel, and the fishing boats have all but disappeared. The new landing is used exclusively by the large ferries which transport passengers to and from North Shields, just across the River Tyne. Several of the old waterfront taverns have disappeared, including the old Coble Inn and the Ferry Tavern. The Alum Ale House still thrives, however, and provides refreshment for thirsty travellers from both sides of the water.

Ivor Muncey

According to some records, the Burton House tavern, owned by Sistersons, was once located in King Street at the other side of the Market Square. However, some time after 1871 the name (and almost certainly the license) was transferred to another inn beside the Ferry Landing. The Burton House was often the last port of call for ferry passengers as it stood directly opposite the gantry. In this picture, four youths and a man look on as the ferry, just visible, hoves into view on the river.

The creation of the new ferry landing, to the west, involved the demolition of numerous buildings that were either in the way or had become surplus to requirements. Sadly, the Burton House was one of them. Where the Burton House stood there is now simply neatly manicured grass, although there are constant rumours that this now verdant expanse will soon be redeveloped. It would be nice to think that the Burton House might go through a third incarnation and once again add to the ambiance of the riverside. However, as traditional inns are currently shutting at the rate of seven per day, this might be nothing more than wishful thinking.

Just how close the Burton House was to the river can be seen from this old photograph taken from the water. A short flight of steps can be seen leading up to the street. These were used by fishermen whose cobles were roped to the wooden gantry on the left. To the right, just out of camera, was the ferry landing itself. The stout anchoring chain can be seen wrapped around a post at the bottom of the photograph.

The streets that led from the ferry landing were "working streets", and, although picturesque, were not always the cleanest of places. Some streets survived, including the quite grandiose Daltons Lane near the Customs House a little further down the river. Daltons Lane was allegedly named after Sir Robert de Dalton, the chaplain of St Hilda's church (or St. Hild's, as it was called then) adjacent to Market Square. Dalton took up his chaplaincy in the year 1322.

Marshall's Quay was one of several places on the riverbank where cobles and larger boats could be repaired quickly. Here, in 1892, a workman can be seen attending to a small coble, replacing a piece of planking which has either come loose or rotted. A man in the background, possibly the vessel's owner, watches with interest. At the top of the steps in the centre of the photograph, washing can be seen blowing in the river breeze.

In 1824, gas lighting was finally introduced to South Shields, and a gas lamp can be seen hanging prominently on the wall in the alley.

Some of the buildings at Marshall's Quay dated back to the early eighteenth century, but by the late nineteenth century were already in a state of disrepair. Relatively few buildings of the type seen here, with the stepped arches over the windows, survived into the twenty-first century, but one, pictured here at King Street, still stands and pays tribute to the architectural grace of a bygone age.

R. Hodge/South Tyneside Libraries

Fishing has always been a popular pastime in South Shields, and in this picture, apparently taken in South Shields, 1928, two anglers can be seen taking a break between catches. The location of the river is uncertain, but may be the River Don close to Tyne Dock after flooding, as it certainly isn't that wide now. Its also highly unlikely that they'd have had much success, but who knows – they might just have got lucky.

Sea fishing is also popular in South Shields, and at times somewhat perilous when the North Sea is behaving tempestuously. Those who prefer a more clement environment often gather at the landing next to the Customs house at the Mill Dam to fish. Later they might pop into the nearby Steamboat, Waterfront or Riverside for a quick pint before taking their supper home.

Shipbuilding always had a major influence in South Shields until recent years, and the decline of "the yards" has seen a great move towards alternative forms of employment. This old illustration shows the site of the West Dock shipyard in 1850, with the ever-present fishermen's cobles in the foreground. However, the twentieth century saw the smaller yards give way to the huge, industrialised complexes and the creation of colossal ships for both the Merchant and Royal Navies.

On both sides of the Tyne many of the old shipyards have disappeared, leaving the land free for more environmentally friendly redevelopment. Although the reduction in the shipping industry on Tyneside has been much lamented, the environmental impact on the river has been a positive one.

Some yards, like McNulty's Offshore, have survived and diversified into oil and gas fabrication, providing much-needed employment. The second picture shows the impressive Northern Producer rig in the Tyne for attention.

Boat-building on the river still takes place on a small scale, much of it accomplished by dedicated enthusiasts.

South Tyneside Libraries

The vessel seen here began life as the *HMS Diamond* a 20-gun sailing brig which served in the Crimean War but was converted into a mission ship at South Shields twelve years later. Stripped of her guns and masts, and renamed *Joseph Straker* after a local shipbuilder, the ship provided comfort and support for upwards of 400 local seafarers. Under the guidance of a chaplain called Garland, the mission ship played host to a temperance club, a reading room, a chess club and a chapel.

By 1882 the ship was showing signs of structural damage, and for this and other reasons it was felt that a more permanent, land-based premises would be better. Two years later the *Seamen's Mission* – now called the *Mission to Seafarers* opened for business at 53 Mill Dam, where it remains to this day.

The mission ship is long gone, and now much larger vessels grace the River Tyne. Seen here is the *Rotterdam*, a ferry of the Holland America Line, as she leaves the river in the summer of 2008 with a full complement of holidaymakers.

The war dead of South Shields have always been shown great respect. Here, a number of old soldiers are gathered around a memorial, although I have been unable to find its exact location and I suspect it no longer stands. It may have been erected in Westoe Cemetery, although the heavy shrubbery and large trees are difficult to place.

The memorial is in the shape of a Celtic Cross, and two of the men in the picture are wearing Glengarry berets, which hints at a Scots connection and only adds to the mystery.

The strong link between South Shields and the ocean makes it only fitting that "those in peril on the sea" were also honoured when their lives were taken from them. The second picture shows a statue unveiled by the Countess Mountbatten of Burma in 1990, in memory of "the thousands of merchant seamen who sailed from this port and lost their lives in World War II".

The sailor at the wheel stares intently at the river, his mouth turned down and his facial muscles taut, as he guides his vessel to some unknown destination. We have much to thank them for.

The erection of a Customs House in the town came as something of a blessing, as previously all business was conducted from Newcastle. After many legal shenanigans and false starts, two Customs Officers were permanently stationed in South Shields in 1848, although contemporary records show that a number of "Preventives" were first housed there on a semi-official basis decades earlier.

The foundation of the Customs House was laid in 1863, having been designed by the local borough surveyor, a Mr. Clemence. The cost of erecting the building was a (now) paltry £3,000.

The Customs House still stands, and is now a vibrant theatre, cinema and centre for the arts. Modern extensions have changed the character of the building considerably, but the original facement can still be seen substantially as it was. The Customs House is now a registered charity, and has proved to be a hugely successful venture as it draws tourists like a magnet from all over the world.

The Old Town Hall was erected in the Market Square in the year 1768, and was allegedly constructed by a local builder named Hunter.

The purpose of the building was to facilitate Court hearings and to provide office space for town officials, although there was precious little space inside. Provision was also made for stallholders to shelter in the Town Hall if the weather became too inclement. The design of what is now referred to as "the Old Town Hall" is aesthetically pleasing and exudes a sense of solidity and permanence. Today it still rests upon the same, stout stone pillars that were there at the beginning and houses the Market Superintendent's office below in what is alleged to have been a holding cell for ne'er-do-wells.

Today, the Old Town Hall remains one of the most fascinating buildings in the town and the market beneath it thrives. The main building is no longer used permanently, but is in a state of good repair and is often hired by local community groups when they stage events.

King Street is the main shopping thoroughfare in the town and still attracts thousands of visitors on a daily basis, although there are continual complaints that business is not as good as it was. The first picture shows King Street as seen from the steps of the Old Town Hall in Market Square whilst the tram service was in operation, hence the tram tracks which are clearly visible in the foreground of the photograph.

The street has changed little over the years, although it is now pedestrianised and the staid, Victorian architecture has given ground to the quick-fit, multi-coloured hoardings of our own time.

Nevertheless, there is no doubt that a resident of the town from one hundred years ago would have little difficulty in recognising King Street today.

One interesting feature is the railway bridge that can be seen traversing the street in the older picture. Although not visible in the second picture it still stands and now it serves the Nexus Metro system which takes passengers all over Tyneside and Wearside.

Another view of King Street, looking towards Market Square and the Old Town Hall which can be seen in the distance on both pictures. Only four horse-and-carts traps can be seen the entire length of the street in the older picture. Later, traffic congestion would become a real problem, leading to eventual pedestrianisation. As the new photograph clearly shows, there is no shortage of pedestrians on a busy Saturday afternoon.

One of the large differences between King Street then and now is the current absence of public houses. Time was when there were over a dozen public houses in the street, not counting those in Market Square. These included *The Bridge Hotel*, *The Golden Lion*, *The King's Head* and *The Lord Collingwood*. The lack of emphasis on alcohol consumption in King Street has made it a more family-friendly place now, but there is still no shortage of restaurants and cafés in the vicinity.

King Street in the late nineteenth century. Notice the single-storey building in the centre of the photograph adjacent to the site of The Golden Lion public house. All buildings in King Street now have two storeys at least.

Also clearly visible in the first picture is one of the old gas lamps, which were later replaced by electric lighting. Just visible on the left of the picture is Bradley's the Tailors, which disappeared many moons ago but was replaced by Burtons and other clothing companies.

The new picture illustrates well how the surviving buildings from the Victorian era have been well maintained, playing host to a wide variety of specialist shops selling mobile phones, games consoles and other luxuries that we have come to take for granted.

As can be seen in the older photograph, handcarts were a common sight, mainly being used to deliver perishable goods such as meat, fish, fruit and vegetables to retailers on a daily basis.

St. Hilda's Church as seen from Market Square looking down Keppel Street. The gable-end store just behind the street lamp on the left of the picture later became a well-known public house called *The Mermaid's Tale*. The pub is still there, although its now known as *Rosie Malone's* – an Irish theme-pub renowned for its good beer and hospitality.

St. Hilda's – formerly called St. Hild's – is a church of great age with a long and venerable history. The tower hosts an imposing clock which had a reputation for regularly breaking down, although Shields folk saw this as a minor inconvenience.

The south face of the building has lost its charm, as the once ostentatious windows have now been blocked up. However, the north side, as seen here, is still picturesque.

The church has been the centre of a number of headline-grabbing incidents over the years – one chap in the nineteenth century was just prevented from throwing himself from the tower by the prompt action of the police and some locals – but today provides a valuable resource for the community and, of course, a place of worship.

This longer shot of Keppel Street still shows St. Hilda's clearly, but notice the *Lifeboat Bar* on the extreme left. *The Lifeboat* was one of the more "respectable" alehouses in the town centre, and was popular with sailors.

As the reader can see from the recent photograph, taken from almost exactly the same position, Keppel Street has been widened considerably as it is now the main bus route through the town centre. The handcarts are gone, along with the tramlines, and one doesn't often see groups of labourers carrying spades crossing the road now, either.

The old buildings behind St. Hilda's Church have now been replaced by a modern retail development and a Job Centre. They lack the architectural elaboration of their predecessors, but most locals would agree that the street has been enhanced by their fresh, sharp appearance.

The Lifeboat Bar? Long gone, I'm afraid. The entire block was demolished to make way for an office-cum-retail development, which itself may eventually be removed due to plans to redevelop the riverside and surrounding area.

The older photograph shows the entrance to South Shields Magistrates Court in Keppel Street, as seen from East Street.

Adjoining the Magistrates Court was Keppel Street Police Station, a large structure that was first home to the South Shields Borough Police and then, later, Northumbria Police into which the old Borough police were incorporated.

By the 1980s, the Keppel Street complex, already the headquarters of Northumbria Police "E Division" – E standing for Echo – housed a Scientific Aids Unit, a Crime Prevention Department and numerous other specialist outfits. Alas, the cost of maintaining an impressive but dilapidated building became too much and the entire structure was pulled down. It must also be said that the changing face of both policing and the administration of justice had made the complex essentially impractical for its intended purpose.

Northumbria Police South Tyneside Command Unit is now housed in a state-of-the-art station at Millbank, Station Road. The new Law Courts – equally as impressive – are at nearby Secretan Way.

W.Parry/South Tyneside Libraries

Commonly referred to as "Barclay's Corner", both photographs show the changing face of the junction of King Street and Mile End Road. The Haircutting Rooms has now been replaced with the far more imposing premises of Barclays Bank. The corner of *The Scotia* public house can be seen on the extreme right of the older image, although the pub itself was later extensively remodelled.

On the recent photograph bollards can be seen. These were added after the street was pedestrianised to prevent illicit traffic, although they can be lowered to facilitate entry by the emergency services and some delivery vehicles. After the first photograph was taken tram tracks were laid. These were removed before the pedestrianisation programme.

In a later picture in this book, taken from the same location, it can be seen that King Street was subsequently widened considerably.

The juncture of Keppel Street and Fowler Street, looking towards Mile End Road. On the older picture (1910), the premises of A. Wetherell & Son, butchers, can be seen. One puzzle concerns the "White Star" logo above the entrance. Its possible that the premises may have been a public house of that name before the Wetherell's took over and they simply used the already existing name as a trading device.

For some reason the attention of Mr. Wetherell, two young delivery boys and several others seems focused intently upon something taking place on the other side of the street, but unfortunately the camera doesn't declare what.

The older photograph enables us to see a number of details concerning the interior of the butchery, including a stout wooden counter, a till and rabbits hanging in the window. A number of posters advertising a local circus can be also be seen on display.

In the recent picture the butcher's has been replaced by Coral the bookmakers, above which is the well-established firm of Hannay & Hannay, Solicitors.

W.Parry/South Tyneside Libraries

The Free Library & Reading Rooms was one of numerous efforts made by the South Shields Borough to provided educational facilities for residents. First opened in 1873, the facility proved to be so popular it was also used as a museum.

In 1888 a fiercely-debated motion was put forward to allow the library to open on Sundays, but in a public poll the suggestion was heavily defeated. Nevertheless, by the later half of the nineteenth century the premises were no longer big enough, so permission was given for the library to use the public hall on the floor above, which effectively doubled its floor space.

In 1898 the extended library and museum was formerly opened by Mr. J. C. Stevenson.

Today the library is located in nearby Prince Georg Square, although at this time of writing the future of the new building is in doubt due to structural problems.

The old premises is now a well-kept and vibrant museum which has proved to be a great attraction for residents and tourists alike, and has just undergone a major refit.

Almost directly opposite the Library & Reading Rooms sat the old Marine School, which provided first-class training for mariners and engineers. The school was opened by Dr. Thomas Winterbottom in 1837. The tower of the building was topped by a magnificent dome. However, as can be seen from the recent photograph this was later removed.

Eventually the function of the Marine School was transferred to the South Shields Marine & Technical College, and the building is now a popular drinking establishment called *The Kirkpatrick*, after soldier James Simpson Kirkpatrick who, with his trusty donkey Murphy, rescued dozens of wounded troops fighting in Turkey during World War I. A statue of both Kirkpatrick and Murphy stands opposite *The Kirkpatrick* as a memorial to this heroic serviceman.

As can be seen by the recent photograph, the façade of the building remains almost perfectly intact and the current owners have made great efforts to protect the integrity of one of the town's most picturesque buildings.

In this earlier snapshot of Barclay's Corner, at the junction of King Street and Mile End Road, a police officer can be seen, possibly directing traffic, although there certainly wasn't much of it. The haircutting rooms are still there, although the general dealers below now shares its premises with H. Davidson, Pawnbrokers and Commission Agent.

Also in the older picture, a horse-drawn cab belonging to the South Shields Transport Company can be seen turning into King Street. The wording of the livery on the side of the cab indicates that its regular route runs between Westoe Village and the Market Square.

In the new picture the full results of the pedestrianisation programme can be seen, with the crossroads between Mile End Road, Ocean Road, Fowler Street and King Street having been turned into a large plaza. Although opposed by some at the time, the change has created a much safer environment for shoppers and the crossroads is often utilised in the summer by entertainers.

In this fascinating 1901 snap of Burrow Street, just off Fowler Street, we can see one of a number of premises owned by Eastman's Ltd, who sold everything from chocolate to grilled beef, milled seeds to American cigars and tea to handkerchiefs.

South Shields in the early part of the twentieth century played host to an incredible array of general dealers who, as well as providing the staples of life, would also have their own specialities. One product Eastman's was well-known for stocking was curry powder which they sold in several different strengths.

Superficially Burrow Street looks radically different now, but appearances can be deceiving. Curry powder can't be purchased there now, but the premises formerly occupied by Eastman's now plays host to a well-established pizzeria and the street holds not one but two Asian restaurants – all of which support the town's reputation for being the best place to find Continental and Eastern cuisine in the north of England.

The corner of Thomas Street, as seen from the opposite side of Fowler Street. What was formerly a vacant lot is now occupied by a household furniture company. The YMCA building just around the corner is still there, although the YMCA has now moved its base of operations to Cookson House on River Drive.

Advertisements on the gable end of Burrow Street encourage the purchase of the laundry detergent Oxydol – still available if you know where to look – and two plays currently being delivered at a local theatre. *Four Pure Girls* starred Sid Field, a well-known comedian, and *The Bashful Boys* highlighted the acting talents of Evelyn Taylor who later became a successful agent to a number of well-known singing stars.

In the older picture both Fowler Street and Thomas Street are cobbled, but in the recent photograph they have been replaced entirely with bitumen and a baffling array of white lines.

The corner of Albermarle Street and Fowler Street, 1901. One of the best-loved stores in South Shields was that of John W. Henderson, "The Boro' Baker", who sold much more than bread and custard tarts. Also available, as can clearly be seen on the posters, were coffee (priced at one shilling), tea (one shilling and fourpence) and "fresh eggs, all selected".

To the left of Henderson's you can see a drug store and another branch of the aforementioned Eastman's.

In the modern picture Henderson's has been replaced by the Leeds Building Society, a testament to our changing times. Fowler Street now houses a large number of banks, building societies and estate agents, and although this has not met with the approval of many older residents, who remember the days when the streets were filled with "proper shops", they are perhaps a necessary evil.

One interesting feature of the older image is the presence of posters urging residents to "vote for Henderson" in a forthcoming local election in the Bents Ward!

The older picture from 1938 illustrates the gable end of Beach Road as seen from the top of Fowler Street. Five workmen are busy repairing the wall which was damaged when the building behind it was demolished. The overhead network of cables used by the trams can be seen hanging overhead, and the tram tracks themselves are just visible on the ground.

In the new image all the essential features have remained intact, although the old stable/barn has now been converted into a taxi office. To the left is Victoria Hall, then used as a school of dance, below which was an off-license (hence the prominent advert for R.O.L. Whisky).

Victoria Hall is now a restaurant and the purveyance of liquor has been supplanted by the selling of domestic carpets. The ornate dome has lost its crowning glory and the chimney stacks have been reduced in size.

Fowler Street has now been widened and includes a bus stop for the convenience of commuters.

Ivor Muneey

In this second view of the junction of Fowler Street and Beach Road an extraordinary sight greets us; two live elephants and one extremely dead mammoth parading down the centre of the road. Dating the picture is difficult, but it was patently taken before 1910 when the "new" Town Hall was erected. Had the picture been taken post-1910, the Town Hall would have been visible clearly in the background as it is in the new photo.

It is just possible that the picture could have been taken in 1904 when "Buffalo Bill" Cody and his travelling Wild West show stopped briefly in the town before heading off to Sunderland. In his later shows the flamboyant (and wonderfully eccentric) Cody incorporated many features that had nothing to do with the Wild West, and a collection of living and dead pachyderms could well have been amongst them.

Whatever the truth, the good folk of South Shields were obviously enthralled at their presence, and to my knowledge the town has never seen such a spectacle since.

The junction of Charlotte Street and Fowler Street. In the older picture we see "Dr. Armstrong's house", in front of which is a horse and trap. Just underneath the horse can be seen a rather bemused black-and-white terrier. The photo may have been taken in the spring or summer, as at least one of the windows in Dr. Armstrong's residence is open.

When the street was later remodelled, an additional house was erected in what had been Dr. Armstrong's garden, effectively making the doctor's house second in the row as opposed to first.

In the new picture, the former garden now houses Moody & Co. Estate Agents on the ground floor, whilst above is the Wright Building Company.

The sedate horse and trap is no longer seen on the streets of South Shields, and outside of Dr. Armstrong's house, as can be seen on the new photograph, there has now sprung up a number of signs bearing all manner of parking restrictions. What would the good doctor have made of it all?

The New Town Hall. Erected in 1910, the "new" town hall is a monument to post-Victorian grandiosity. Designed by the respected architect Ernest E. Fetch, the new municipal buildings were created within what now seems like the insanely low budget of £45,000. To this day the frontage of the building remains virtually unchanged and is instantly recognisable.

When the tenders for designing the new town hall were first solicited, the local council had the foresight to require a building which could easily be added to as the need arose. There have been a number of major extensions, along with a radical remodelling of the newer section in 2008.

Unlike many buildings of its kind, the town hall has been kept in an excellent state of repair and is still the nerve centre of everything that happens within the Borough of South Tyneside. Although modern conveniences such as elevators have been added, the Borough Council always seems to have to have plotted a sensible course between the sharp rocks of extremist retentionism and unwarranted modernism. Despite the many changes, the building still retains its original character and sense of grandeur.

Ivor Muncey

Garden Lane. In the older picture we are presented with a stereotypical image of working class culture and accommodation; terraced houses, dust and gas lamps. The photographer was looking down form what is now Crossgate towards the town centre as a number of residents go about their business. Although run down to a degree, the street was essentially well kept and contained a number of thriving businesses.

Garden Lane today is hardly recognisable, save for its descending elevation towards the town centre. The road was widened, first in 1932, and then subsequently on several occasions as traffic flow increased and congestion became a problem.

The houses have long since been demolished, of course, but the businesses in Garden Lane are thriving. A brisk walk downhill will bring you into the rapidly changing commercial epicentre where, at this time of writing, one new shopping complex is still finding its feet and another is about to be erected on the site of the old Coronation Street car park.

Claypath Lane. Don't you just love the earthy romanticism of some of those old street names? In the older picture, taken in 1939, five little girls can be seen playing some sort of game which involved joining hands, whilst a woman bedecked in furs and carrying a fashionable bag makes here way across the road.

In the background, two young men – one riding a bike – are engaging in conversation. Just below the centre of the picture a Scottish Terrier seems to be peering tentatively into someone's back yard.

Claypath Lane has changed radically now, of course, and whereas in the 1920s it was relatively traffic-free it now boasts a car park. What was formerly the Chameleon restaurant is now the real ale pub called *The Maltings,* and in the newer picture the Westoe Baptist Church can be seen, still offering spiritual companionship as it has done since its construction in 1881.

Long Row *circa* 1896. The older picture depicts a number of retail premises and one pub, *The Hope & Anchor*, but was better known for its "many common boarding houses and seamen's lodgings". One look at the scene tells its own story; Long Row wasn't exactly the classier part of South Shields.

There are at least 22 people in this photograph, none of them who look well-heeled. One young lad, to the far left and facing away from the camera, is painfully thin and barefooted. A shop in the foreground has its windows covered with old sheeting, perhaps to protect the contents – maybe meat or fish – from exposure to sunlight.

A drink in *The Hope and Anchor* – or one of the other eleven public houses that graced Long Row at the time – was essentially the only form of communal recreation available to locals at the time. Now, as you can see, Long Row is a picturesque drive which bears little resemblance to its former self.

South Tyneside Libraries

Comical Corner, just off Long Row, was a well-known area of South Shields that was reputed to be haunted by a number of spectres, including a retired sea-dog called Jack the Hammer. The stories later inspired a book about the spooky goings-on, which was probably the first literary effort dedicated to the ghosts of South Shields!

The shop to the left of the picture exudes character, and an advertisement for mustard can be seen hanging on an interior wall through the window. Also visible are tinned goods and trays of toffee. The store on the opposite corner sold coffee, which was particularly popular with the Arab seamen.

The rather solemn-looking woman in the foreground, with a shawl over her head, is carrying what appears to be a parcel of meat from the local butchers.

The recent picture shows the entrance to Long Row, which once led to Comical Corner.

East Holborn. The exact date and location of this picture are uncertain, although it was definitely taken in the East Holborn area and probably around 1901. The public houses at the end of the street on the right are probably *The Comfortable* and *The Bottle House*, both registered at 23 East Holborn and ran by one Elizabeth Mason. *The Bottle House* was formerly known as *The Bottle House Tavern*, which opened for business some time before 1871. The pub on the left may well be *The Red Lion*, once managed by Tommy Atkinson.

East Holborn is no longer a bustling community, and has largely been taken over by small-to-medium size businesses. In the newer photograph the "timeless Tyne" can still be seen meandering its way to the North sea. Some things never change.

A rather moving picture of an old sweet shop in Shadwell Street, not surprisingly frequented by no less than ten (honestly, count them) youngsters in this photograph, of varying ages, none of whom look as if they could afford to buy any of the candy on offer inside.

The windows of the old shop are filled with ornate china jars, and the left-hand (facing) window also has a shelf which holds, amongst other things, two soft drink bottles.

The traditional sweet shops are all but gone, but the gap has been more than admirably filled by more sophisticated confectioners such as Thorntons, who now operate in King Street. An interesting sign of the times is that Thorntons now cater for diabetics by offering a wide range of goodies made with reduced sugars and sweeteners – something that the sweet shop proprietors of old, God bless 'em, would never (and could never) have envisioned.

The "baths and washhouse" near Cuthbert Street were erected in 1854 and certainly looked solid enough, but were demolished just half a century later. A number of children can be seen playing in or near the portico, and the baths provided an important social function as bathing facilities in homes were virtually non-existent unless the householders were quite wealthy.

Later, the baths were rebuilt in Derby Terrace, where they remained until the latter half of the twentieth century.

The Derby Terrace baths are gone too, now, and bathers can visit the superb leisure centre at Temple Park which offers bathing facilities that would have been beyond the wildest dreams of the Victorians.

The contrast between the old baths near Cuthbert Street and Temple Park highlight an important cultural difference. Victorian architects loved to create echoes of ancient Rome and Greece by the use of ornate pillars and arches, whereas nowadays we search for modernity and a glimpse of the future.

From the steps of the Town Hall. The vista in the old photograph consists of open spaces and numerous glimpses of a bygone age; the police box in the distance, the old iron and glass bus shelter and motor vehicles that bear little resemblance to those on the road today.

To the left of the picture is a statue of Queen Victoria, which graced Chichester for many decades before being relocated to its current site just outside of the Town Hall.

The new picture of the same location depicts a much busier scene, and every inch of land is utilised to its maximum. The inset shows the statue of Queen Victoria as it is now, just off camera to the left.

The shop fronts in the old photograph can still be seen, but have been radically modernised.

South Tyneside Libraries

The junction of Laygate and Frederick Street, 1906. In the old picture sits a bustling general dealers, and predominant is the sign advertising "Hunt's Botanic Drinks" which were available at the Temperance Bar next door. These largely consisted of ginger beer, dandelion and burdock and sarsaparilla, although other exotic flavours such as elderflower were also available – all without the presence of that perfidious substance known as alcohol, of course.

The same spot now is occupied by Laygate Post Office, one of the most popular stores in the area due largely to the friendly disposition of the proprietors. The ornate frontage of old is gone, and perhaps that's a pity, but the character of the street remains.

In recent times a pedestrianised area with seating has been provided for weary shoppers (foreground) along with strategically placed litter bins and a saucy yellow container which holds road grit ready to be scattered on the ashphalt if and when it should ever snow heavily again.

A view along Laygate. On the left sits a row of shops, including Dowell's the florists and Johnson's dairy, the latter of which prided itself on the sale of "pure" ice cream. To the right of the picture in the background can be seen the corner entrance to the Adam & Eve pub.

As with the old picture of Chichester, the lack of pedestrians is almost breathtaking. Only one person can be seen in the photograph, a young man who appears to be waiting for the dairy to open. Of course, this may indicate that the picture could have been taken very early in the morning which would explain the deserted streets.

In the recent picture, also taken early in the morning, the Adam & Eve can be seen more clearly. Dickson's the butchers and Al's Sandwich Bar are just opening for business, a Post Office van can be seen pulling out of Frederick Street back lane and an early shopper is already making her way home.

David Hutchinson

This fading old photograph depicts a thriving greengrocers in Frederick Street, above which is a huge banner announcing the Diamond Jubilee of Queen Victoria. This dates the picture to June, 1897. Incredibly, the store is still a greengrocers to this day, and in the capable hands of David Hutchinson whose family has traded in "fruit and veg" for four generations.

Quality of merchandise means as much to David as it did to the proprietor over a century ago, but things have changed and attitudes have relaxed a little. As in the recent photograph, visitors to Hutchinsons today will likely see David sporting one of several rather outlandish pieces of headgear, all designed to put a smile on customers' faces.

Another difference – often not appreciated by younger shoppers – is the huge choice of produce available now as opposed to then. You'd certainly have been able to purchase potatoes and apples in 1897 – but definitely not kumquats and kiwi fruits.

Ivor Muncey

Disaster strikes at the Dean Maltings, one of the foremost suppliers of brewing materials in the town. A huge flood engulfed the premises and pretty much everything else in sight. Floods were common in South Shields at that time, and are not unknown today. However, having your business submerged to this degree is a thankfully thing of the past.

The brewing industry largely became extinct in the town, but has recently been revived by the Jarrow Brewery in Claypath Lane which produces an exquisite range of real ales on the premises adjacent to their pub, *The Maltings*. The old "Westoe Brewery" logo can be seen on the outside.

The Jarrow Brewery is on higher ground and unlikely to be flooded, and for that mercy we may be eternally grateful.

At one time there were five other breweries in South Shields; The Holborn Brewery, The High Brewery, The Market Place Brewery, The Waterloo Vale Brewery and the Subscription Brewery, none of which survive today.

South Tyneside Libraries

Another flood, this time at West Park in 1901. Cascades of water can be seen gushing into an area of low elevation, and the shattered remains of the wall and adjacent fences have been taken with it, presenting a stark illustration of the power of Mother Nature. In the background, seven witnesses to the event stand incredulously, watching as the torrent destroys everything in its path.

The same scene today shows that the park is still there, and the houses to the right no longer have to endure such disasters. More efficient drainage and the levelling of the roads have largely removed the threat.

A stone stairwell also graced the corner, allowing pedestrians to descend into the park easily. This too was destroyed in the flood. Access nowadays can be gained by a number of entrances nearby.

Yet another flood at Whitehead Street, Tyne Dock, on October 27, 1900. Bizarrely, six youngsters can be seen in a boat negotiating the waters whilst a crowd of onlookers watches intently in the background.

Whitehead Street and the surrounding environs today have changed radically. The old houses have been demolished, areas of grassland have been built upon and terraced streets have been replaced with flats and maisonettes.

In the background of the recent picture, a young mother walks her child securely fastened in a buggy – both almost certainly unaware of the tempest that once gave the area a radically different appearance to that which now greets visitors.

The intent of the youngsters in the boat is now unknown, although it isn't impossible that they were intending to effect a rescue of some householders who had become trapped in their dwellings.

A picnic at Cleadon Hills. The village of Cleadon lies on the border of South Shields and is now an affluent suburb. The hills nearby are still popular with ramblers, but at one time they were also a magnet for church outings – particularly at Easter time.

In the older picture, taken in 1935, a number of women from (or associated with) Night Street Methodist Chapel in Jarrow can be seen enjoying themselves. In the background a young girl seems to be sipping a cup of tea.

In the more recent picture, taken in 1983, Cleadon Village can be seen in the foreground whilst rain clouds roll ominously overhead.

The women in the photograph are Ethel Mankin (top left facing), Janet Watson, the author's maternal grandmother (top right facing), Polly stewart (bottom left facing) and Jenny Mankin (bottom right facing).

Another picnic at Cleadon, this time almost certainly in the centre of the village by the small but well-known pond. The woman third from the left (facing) is the author's maternal great-grandmother, Elizabeth Trewick.

Behind the revellers can be seen the low wooden fence surrounding the pond, which was probably intended to form some sort of barrier to prevent children getting too close to the water. It is highly unlikely to have been effectual.

In the recent picture, the small grassy bank has been replaced with shrubbery and is somewhat smaller in size, making it impossible to hold a picnic! The fence is still there, however, although it has been renewed several times since the older photograph was taken in the late 1920s.

Other additions to the scene include seating for weary walkers and the now – mandatory road markings.

Although the exact location of the outing in Cleadon cannot be identified with absolute certainty, the pond is the best bet, although even back then it was, I must confess, a rather odd place for a picnic.

What a difference a century can make. The older picture shows an idyllic rural scene that appears far removed from the hustle and bustle of civilisation, and in many respects it was. A lonely footpath stretches between Brinkburn Farm and Harton Colliery, both of which have now disappeared. A rather ragged scarecrow keeps watch over the fields and the tumbledown fences have obviously seen better days.

Virtually all of the surrounding area, including the footpath pictured, have now been developed and parts are buried beneath the imposing edifice of South Tyneside General District Hospital, also pictured.

In the newer picture, parts of the old infirmary which have now been incorporated into the new hospital are shaded by trees which offer only the faintest echo of the verdant countryside which once covered the area. In front lies one of the many well-used car parks and a sign warning that speed is restricted to 10mph. One imagines this would have been uncomfortably fast for the carts of old Brinkburn Farm.

The old Westoe Bridges, which, like Tyne Dock Arches, many people thought would be there forever. It was not to be. The arches are gone, and the bridges long removed.

Although Westoe Bridges were loved by many, it has to be said that their presence was a little claustrophobic. At one time the old Glebe Methodist Church stood like a sentinel nearby, but fashionable new apartments have replaced that, too. The entire effect has been to re-format the landscape into something less than three-dimensional, flatter and open-spaced.

The traffic flow up Westoe Road has increased markedly since the bridges were removed, although there is no direct relationship between the two circumstances. The area certainly looks more up-market.

The builders' truck in the older picture looks positively cartoonesque in comparison to those used today, but one supposes it did the job. The builders themselves, you will note, are all wearing the mandatory flat caps and old suit jackets that were necessary apparel back then just like reflective jackets and hard hats are now.

Looking down Dean Road from Westoe, 1856. A fenced-off tree, *sans* leaves, stands in solitary opposition to the growing urbanisation of the area. The roughly-finished road is covered with a fine blanket of snow, indicating that the picture was taken in wintertime.

On the left of the new picture is the well-known Hedworth Hall, long valued as a place to organise receptions both familial and professional. Hedworth Hall was for a time known as *The Golden Slipper*, prompting some wag to call it *The Yeller Wellie* (for those unfamiliar with the Geordie tongue, *The Yellow Wellington Boot*).

Built in 1925, Hedworth Hall has just undergone a major refit and is enjoying a new lease of life. The rest of Dean Road has also altered considerably, but now, as then, it had a reputation for being a good shopping area.

The old Ingham Infirmary, which in its time treated many wounded soldiers, scores of scraped knees and a disturbing number of other (often alcohol-inspired) injuries.

The Ingham Infirmary possessed stateliness and majesty; as medical skills were ever advancing, the hospital stayed pretty much the same. It provided, to use the old adage, constancy in the midst of change.

Alas, all good things come to an end and the time came when keeping the Ingham open was neither financially viable or practical. Its operations – if you'll excuse the pun – were transferred to the newly renovated and expanded District General Hospital which graciously honoured the memory of its decaying colleague by naming a wing in its memory.

The site of the Ingham Infirmary was developed and is now covered in attractive new homes. Architecturally they are superb and great efforts were made to keep their appearance in character with the old hospital. Indeed, bits of the old infirmary were saved and incorporated into the new estate, as the recent photograph shows.

Ivor Muncey

Just across the road from Ingham Grange is the old *Westoe Hotel*. The *Westoe* formed both a social hub for locals and a retreat for travelling salesmen from distant climes unable to get home for the night. Always renowned for its beer and hospitality, the pub did a brisk business, being situated at the nexus of two busy roads.

The history of the inn is a little confused, and both licences and names seem to have been bandied around somewhat in the mid-to-late nineteenth century. However, the hotel has been an almost constant feature of life in the locality for generations.

The *Westoe* recently underwent a quite rigorous facelift despite the fact that it was always a pretty decent pub on the inside anyway. Westoe had its own brewery at one time, but as mentioned earlier it bit the dust several decades ago. The new Jarrow Brewery has produced three ales in honour of its previous incarnation; Westoe Netty Special, Westoe Lifeboat Ale and Westoe IPA.

Try them; go on, you know you want to...

The area now known as "Westoe Junction" as seen from Horsley Hill Road. In the older picture a general dealers can be seen sporting a variety of comestibles in the window. As one can see in the recent snap, the premises are now occupied by Hogg's the chemist, which sits beneath a rather obvious blue and white painted sign announcing, "NATIONAL HEALTH SERVICE – PRESCRIPTIONS DISPENSED". In the old photograph a horse and cart ambles towards The Westoe Hotel, whilst in the new picture we see the stereotypical white van.

Another sign of the times is the fact that no less than eleven lights, Belisha beacons and bollards are now present in one small area, whilst in the old photograph there are absolutely none.

A pleasing mock-Tudor frontage can be seen on a house in the newer picture, adding a quaintness to the otherwise stark Victorian architecture.

Idyllic Westoe Village in 1865. The features that would come to act as hallmarks of Westoe are already in place, including the wooden rail and the stout walls and robust railings. A tall trellis has been attached to the front of the house on the right to encourage the growth of ivy, which was often used to strategically cover defects in the masonry. This was unlikely to have been the motivation then, however, as the residents of Westoe Village were usually magistrates, politicians or professional people and weren't short of a bob or two to pay the builders.

In 1894 the wooden rail that divides the street was moved to allow easier access, but it is still visible in the new picture. Some of the ornate brick walls surrounding the gardens have been removed over the last 140 years and replaced with railings, although this has done little to alter the character of Westoe.

Westoe Village in 1889. Westoe Village is an oasis of calm in a busy world, playing host to a number of stately buildings. One – 5, Westoe Village – was the birthplace of William Fox who came into this world in 1812. Fox later served four separate terms as Prime Minister of New Zealand, and the house he was born in is now a hotel bearing his name.

In the older picture, a solitary chap can be seen leaning against the wooden railings that have characterised Westoe Village for so long. It is interesting to see that three bollards are already present in the street to reduce traffic and encourage pedestrianisation.

In the recent picture the bollards have been removed and vehicles have, as can be seen, easy access to the street.

A feature in both pictures are the trees which have always been a pleasing feature of Westoe, although from time-to-time they have tended to uplift nearby paving stones and required maintenance.

A rather haunting image of a woman walking uphill on her own. The location of the picture is unclear, although we know that it was taken in South Shields in 1901. The style of the buildings to her left hint that it might have been taken near one of the salt panns, although we cannot be certain. Another possible location is Sunderland Road. Her dress, a conservative black, is tied with a cord around the waist and she wears a chequered, tasselled scarf over her head.

In the second picture, eerily reminiscent of the first, a woman walks uphill at the rear of Fowler Street, adjacent to the municipal car park, in the direction of Saville Street. The only thing that separates the two scenes is the clothing of the subject, as in the modern picture post-Victorian conservative apparel has been replaced by slacks and a casual jacket.

A horse and cart ambles through the streets of South Shields, just behind a horse-drawn taxi cab. A close look at the roadway behind shows that these horses – or others like them – were not averse to leaving the odd "calling card" here and there as they went about their masters' business.

The only horse-drawn carts usually seen nowadays – and they are becoming increasingly rare – are those that belong to scrap merchants who journey in from outside the borough.

South Tyneside Libraries

In the second picture we see a magnificent carriage bearing the livery of Ringtons, the legendary north east tea and coffee merchants who have delivered their wares to the good folk of South Shields for over a century now. These days deliveries are normally made in vans – still bearing the distinctive Ringtons colours – but the carriage is still brought out for special occasions. The smiling Ringtons employee is Victoria Johnson who helped organise the firm's centenary in 2007.

South Shields harbour in 1889. A dark and brooding illustration of the South Shields riverway painted over 100 years ago. A variety of ships and boats, ranging from small cobbles to clippers can be seen at various points on the river.

The River Tyne in the nineteenth century could be a dangerous place, and in the foreground several treacherous eddies are visible.

The new picture, taken from near the landing of the South Shields ferry, shows a rather more idyllic scene. Two large ships are visible, but basking in much calmer waters as the sunlight cascades over the river.

To the left of the picture tall cranes from North Tyneside shipyards intrude upon the skyline.

The River Tyne is far cleaner now than it used to be, a circumstance which has seen salmon return to parts of the waterway they had previously abandoned. The older picture may be filled with the essence of river life over a century ago, but no one should delude themselves that all was sweetness and light when the heavens opened and the winds blew.

A picture depicting the wreck of the passenger ship *Stanley* in 1864. On November 24 of that year, during ferocious storms, the Aberdeen-based passenger steamer came to grief on an area known as the Black Middens with terrible loss of life. A rescue boat bravely attempted to rescue some passengers, and partially succeeded, but was itself sunk. All the women on board the boat, plus one crewman, perished in the waves. Another ship, *Friendship*, was also wrecked that night.

In the older, graphic depiction of the sinking, on the other side of the river, just right of centre, stands the remains of Tynemouth Priory. In the recent snap, taken by the author from the south side of the river at South Shields, at dusk, the priory can also be seen.

Tynemouth Priory – or what is left of it – hasn't changed at all. Shipping on the Tyne has advanced a great deal, however, and tragedies like the wreck of the *Stanley* thankfully fall somewhere between rare and non-existent.

William Wouldhave was born in 1751 and first came to attention in the town, if not prominence, as the clerk of St. Hilda's Church. Wouldhave's entry into the history books was due to his invention of the modern lifeboat – a claim which has not gone unchallenged, as some believe the credit should go to Lionel Lukin.

In the older picture, taken in 1910, the original lifeboat can be seen on display in a purpose-built stand. As can be seen in the recent picture, the boat is currently on display today in Sea Road, although the paint is a different colour. The stand is the original, only the roof having been replaced when the first eventually succumbed to the elements.

Wouldhave, a man with a bit of a temper and a rather colourful vocabulary, died a pauper in his home at the Mill Dam. He was seventy years old. He was a mercurial character, but he (and Lionel Lukin) both left a legacy that would save many, many lives.

The older photograph (*circa* 1921), which was damaged and has been digitally restored, shows a number of fishing baskets photographed on the coast at South Shields, although the exact location cannot be determined. Beside them sits a boat of unknown ownership.

Sea fishing has always been closely connected with South Shields, and river fishing is still extremely popular too. The second photograph shows a number of boats in storage near the coast. Yachting is a pass-time still engaged in by locals.

The South Shields Sailing Club is now over fifty years old and has hosted a number of competitions. It is based near the Groyne at Littlehaven Beach and stoutly maintains a marine heritage that has been with the town since its inception.

The treacherous North Sea has been responsible for many deaths, and contemporary records from the nineteenth century are littered with tragedies, particularly the sinking of small boats in the vicinity of Marsden Bay.

Evelyn Waugh-Almond

Marsden Bay at the turn of the twentieth century. On the left can be seen Marsden Rock, a towering edifice which is synonymous with this beautiful stretch of coastline. The rock was well known for the huge arch which once cut through its centre, but a collapse in 1996 altered its appearance forever. The arch fell to the ground, and the southerly pillar was demolished for health and safety reasons. The larger northern aspect is still standing.

To the right of the picture can be seen the *Marsden Grotto Inn,* a public house built in a cave which was created by one of the area's most enigmatic characters, the Scotsman Peter Allan.

In the recent picture, taken at dusk, a gull can be seen hovering over a choppy sea. *The Marsden Grotto Inn* is still standing, although it now sports a lift shaft which takes visitors down to the pub from the cliff top up above.

Marsden Bay is still incredibly popular with tourists, and presents some of the most beautiful coastal scenery in the UK.

Bathing at Marsden. Taken in 1941, the older photograph shows a mother and child at the water's edge. The woman is drawing her son's attention to something further up the beach, and we can only speculate at what. In the background a second child engages in the age-old ritual of "plodging", whilst in the distance a boat containing three people rides the choppy sea.

The newer photograph was taken in 1985. Again, mother and son have been swimming. The ever-present gulls can be seen foraging in the background amongst the detritus brought in by the tide.

Although both photographs depict happy times, bathing at South Shields is not something that should be engaged in frivolously. The tides can be dangerous, and lives have been lost when bathers have suddenly been swept out to sea.

In recent years it has become fashionable to engage in "charity dips" – often held on New Year's Day – to raise money for worthy beneficiaries. Hardy souls will brave the freezing waters, sometimes dressed in outlandish costumes, but its all in a good cause.

Souter Lighthouse at Whitburn – a well-known tourist attraction – no longer guides in ships but it is still open as a museum and visitor centre. Although not strictly within the precincts of South Shields it is intrinsically connected with the town. It was built in 1871 and was the most sophisticated structure of its time. The upper picture is a watercolour of the lighthouse and several attached buildings in the foreground.

The second photograph shows Souter Lighthouse from a distance painted in striking red and white. Below one can see the original dwellings which now house a shop, restaurant, museum and other educational facilities for visitors.

Ivor Muncey

The older photograph, of uncertain age, was seemingly taken in West Holborn. They say every picture tells a story, and this one is no exception: Down-at heel frontages, boarded up shops and ragged posters peeling from walls all paint a picture of grinding poverty. In the bottom left-hand corner a young man hovers aimlessly, although perhaps he's waiting for a pal to arrive, who knows.

The second picture shows West Holborn today. A residential terrace looks out over the waterfront, whilst in the distance towering cranes testify to the fact that there are still jobs to be had in traditional industries.

The riverside at South Shields is constantly changing, and one benefit is the increased attention being given to environmentally – friendly means of development. Too late for those who endured great hardship over a century ago, of course – but a distinct blessing to the town's residents now.

Caroline Sanderson

The South Marine Park. A jewel in the crown of South Shields, the park has proved a picturesque attraction to thousands. Well-kept stretches of grass and beautifully manicured shrubbery blend tastefully with architectural conveniences such as the plaza which overlooks the rest of the park.

In the first picture, taken in 1905, visitors can be seen sitting in the sun and enjoying themselves. One holds a parasol, indicating that she may have found the heat too much. A young man looks up at the camera curiously, not realising that he would be immortalised in the pages of a book over a century later!

The second picture shows the same location today. The park is just as attractive, and has been enhanced by the addition of a number of statues. One of these can be seen on the extreme left of the new photograph, partially hidden by the branches of a nearby tree.

Fore! Well, maybe that's getting a little carried away, but the putting green in the North Marine Park was an incredibly popular attraction until quite recently. Back in the Sixties, for threepence one could hire a club and a ball, plus a sheet of paper to keep your score on.

Ethel Mankin and Jane Watson can be seen in the old photograph (*circa* 1942) preparing to tee off at the eighteenth hole, their smiles disguising the formidable degree of competition that could colour putting rivalry between friends.

The putting green has gone now, replaced by a more natural display of lawn and shrubbery in the park which, like the South Marine Park on the opposite side of the road, is truly a place of beauty.

Bob Watson

Taken in 1910, the older photograph shows the entrance to the South Shields fairground. A roller-coaster of great complexity dominates the picture, whilst a diminutive ice-cream stall can be seen below. A policeman on a bicycle can be seen riding past in the foreground, whilst another cyclist follows behind. On the other side of the road a third cyclist has stopped to catch his breath whilst a young woman, also with a bike, seems to be pondering whether to chance her arm and have a go upon the death-defying ride.

In the recent photograph the new roller-coaster can be seen, highly decorated in a wide variety of colours. Beside the entrance a large sign advertises another modern distraction; that of go-karting.

The fairground at South Shields has provided fun and enjoyment for families since the late nineteenth century, and according to reports at this time of writing is about to undergo a radical modernisation which will provide a wider variety of attractions .

In past decades travelling circuses and menageries regularly visited South Shields. In the older photograph (*circa* 1943) two uniformed keepers show off a young chimpanzee to a crowd of onlookers. One young chap has confidently taken the simian by the hand and doesn't seem in the least scared of being bitten. To be honest, the chimp looks as if it is basking in the attention.

The second photograph shows the entrance to Uncle Sam's American Circus which still visits the town annually.

Circus acts involving animals are quite rare now due to concerns expressed by animal rights activists, and have largely been replaced by more creative displays of acrobatics and clowning by humans.

I personally visited Uncle Sam's Circus in 2007 when it came to South Shields – the first I'd ever attended in my life – and must confess to being impressed. The high-wire acts looked truly dangerous, and I came perilously close to being squirted with water by an engaging clown called Ramone.

Other circuses also visit the borough on a regular basis, and contain an increasing number of Eastern European performers who, it has to be said, really know how to put on a show.

The changing face of housing. This old picture, taken in Wapping Street *circa* 1900, graphically illustrates the poor quality of many of the town's buildings at that time. Plaster has crumbled extensively from the walls, exposing the brickwork underneath, and several windows are boarded up completely or in a poor state of repair.

Also in the photograph, the poverty endemic in parts of the town is highlighted by the shoddy clothing worn by the young lad gazing up the stairwell on the left. His trousers appear to have been darned and patched in numerous places and his jacket looks to be several sizes too small, indicating that it probably was a hand-me-down.

In the new picture, taken in Greathead Street, older housing has now been extensively renovated and the preponderance of satellite dishes speaks of new-found financial freedom, if not wealth. The majority of windows are now manufactured from UPVC as opposed to wood, and none of them are boarded up or broken.

The author's maternal grandfather, Bob Watson, and his great uncle David Trewick (foreground) enjoying a day out at the coast. The bubbled, complex limestone indicates that the photograph was taken to the north of Marsden Bay at the area generally known as Velvet Beds.

In the new photograph, the author is pictured standing in front of some rocks at approximately the same location.

Until recently, "trips" to the coast were a substitute for holidays in farther climes which were only affordable to a few. It was quite common for day-trippers to walk to South Shields from Jarrow, Hebburn or even further afield to save a few coppers that would otherwise be spent on public transport.

Velvet Beds was a popular picnic area until the 1940s, but erosion of the rock and the diminution of the grassy areas have largely brought the practice to a halt. Still, judging by the smiles on their faces a good time was had by all...

The Ferry Tavern public house which once stood adjacent to the ferry landing in South Shields. The inn had a mercurial history and vacillated between being a lively pub known for its good food and music and a down-at-heel beer bar to be avoided by discerning drinkers.

Shortly before it was demolished, in 2001, the pub ironically saw an upturn in its fortunes and was once again a fun place to socialise. Alas, as can be seen in the more recent picture, this change in fortune was short-lived.

There is an interesting ghost story attached to the *Ferry Tavern*. Some passers-by reported seeing a "Victorian waif" - a young girl aged around nine or ten – standing outside the pub's entrance. She would, allegedly, disappear after a few seconds. One tale is that she was drowned in the river after waiting unsuccessfully for her mother who was drinking in a nearby pub.

The County Hotel at Westoe. The County is a vibrant drinking den immensely popular with students from the nearby South Tyneside College.

In the older photograph, taken in 1910, three riders on horseback can be seen heading in the direction of Westoe Village. Four young lads can be seen emerging from the rear of the inn, having possibly been engaging in mischief. An older girl, heading in the opposite direction, is rolling a hoop in front of her.

As can be seen from the recent photograph, *The County Hotel* has changed little over the last century. The road is now neatly covered with ashphalt and buildings cover what were once open spaces. Street lights have been erected, and Sunderland Road is now a dual carriageway in places.

Through it all *The County Hotel* has stood as a silent witness to the relentless march of progress whilst stubbornly refusing to compromise its reputation for serving a really good pint.

Ivor Muncey

The Hop Pole was a smuggler's pub on the riverside, and had a notorious reputation. It was the scene of several murders and reputedly had a ghost known as The Red Lady who would, allegedly, lean out of an upstairs window and scream in the most blood-curdling fashion at passing ships. Legend had it that if The Red Lady pointed at a ship it would ultimately sink shortly thereafter.

At one point a Roman Catholic priest was alleged to have carried out an exorcism at the premises – or at least attempted to, but was traumatised by an encounter with a spectre in a locked room, after which it took him some considerable time to recover.

Likely The Red Lady was an artifice invented by the smugglers to frighten away the Excise Men and other unwanted visitors, as the huge pub has a foreboding look about it. In the background one can see signs of shipbuilding taking place on the north side of the river.

The second photograph shows the riverbank at night. The Hop Pole is gone but the hallmarks of industrial activity are still there.

The Turk's Head was a well-loved public house near the Lawe Top area of the town. In its hey-day it had an unassailable reputation for providing live music as well as good beer. A "free house", the pub was said to sell more Tetley's Bitter than any other establishment in the locale. Whether this was true I don't know.

At the back of *The Turk's Head* there used to be a long flight of stairs as can be seen in the older picture. For many years rumours abounded that there was also a "secret tunnel" that led from the cellar of the pub, and that it had At one time been used by the press gangs and/or smugglers. Some claimed that *The Turk's Head* stood on the site of an earlier building and that the tunnel had originally been connected to the previous premises, although I have not been able to verify this.

The more recent photograph was taken in 2001, before the pub was demolished. Many local patrons of the establishment were sorry indeed to see it go.

South Tyneside Libraries

The older picture is of Thrift Street, showing the Silent Woman public house (you'd never get away with a name like that nowadays) and the Pollard cooperage.

Three young barefooted "urchins" can be seen walking towards the photographer, one of them partially obscured by a miner clutching his pipe as he makes his way home from work. His face is blackened with coal dust to an almost comical degree. An older, silver-haired chap is making his way up the bank with a large parcel under his arm. We can only guess at its contents.

The Silent Woman did a brisk trade with workmen as it was on a main thoroughfare. *The Brigantine* public house, as seen in the new picture, fulfils a similar role today as it sits in the alley which connects Ferry Street to then Market Square. *The Brigantine* closed recently, which was sad, but quickly opened up again under new management. Let's hope it stays that way.

Ivor Muncey

Kennedy's Bar at Tyne Dock is one of the town's most venerated drinking establishments. As the earlier photograph shows, it stood alone at one time as a prominent landmark. The pub was later renamed *The Dock Hotel*, but nostalgia eventually dictated that the original name was restored in honour of the first proprietor, John Kennedy. It still bears that name today.

One of the perennial problems faced by the pub is flooding. The bar sits in a natural dip which, when the weather is particularly inclement, is transformed almost magically into something akin to a miniature version of the Pacific Ocean. I exaggerate, of course, but the problem is really serious and numerous photographs of the pub, up to is proverbial waist in water, are in circulation.

Kennedy's Bar is one of the few remaining authentic beer bars in the town, now, and has resisted all attempts to transform it into a psychedelic wine bar or glitzy purveyor of over-priced exotic cocktails.
Long may it prosper.

The Scotia is one of the best-known pubs in the town, sitting on the corner of King Street and Mile End Road. The bar has undergone a number of radical transformations over the years and is now virtually unrecognisable when compared to the original.

Popular with visiting seamen in the 1930s, the bar developed a reputation for selling a wide range of good quality spirits.

The Scotia is a splendid bit of architecture, and visitors who fail to study the building in its entirety may well miss the rather magnificent tower which sits atop the roof. Parts of the upper aspect of the building are now inaccessible, but the bar itself, on the ground floor, hosts two entrances – one in King Street itself and the other around the corner in Mile End Road.

One old tale connected with the pub suggests that, back in the 1920s, a drinker got locked in after hours and was found two days later in the roof unconscious. How he got there no one knows. Is the story true? Not a bit of it, methinks, but its a great yarn...

Ye Olde Sportsman started life in 1891 as part of the old Assembly Rooms, eventually became a pub in it's own right and was given the name *The North Eastern* after the railway company whose trains used the adjacent line quite literally across the road.

For the better part of a century the pub remained unchanged, but in the 1990s the owners, Scottish & Newcastle Breweries, revamped the place and renamed it *Ye Olde Sportsman*. One of the central features was a larger-than-life model of a rugby player, and sporting memorabilia covered much of the walls.

Several years ago the new owners renovated the place completely – it was badly in need of it – and the result was the swish *Manhattan's*. I'm not normally in favour of modernising old bars, but I'm happy to make an exception in this case. The food served there is second to none, and if you're keen on having a good DJ or enjoy a spot of karaoke, *Manhattan's* is your place.

The older picture, taken just across the road from *The Scotia*, shows the junction of Fowler Street and Ocean Road. To the right is *The Criterion* – still there – although then it was advertised prominently as a "Restaurant & Grill".

In the background, on the other side of Ocean Road, can be seen the corner of *The Ship & Royal* – also still there – although the frontage of the building has changed radically. The tobacconist on the extreme right of the picture has long gone and currently the jewellers Warren James occupies the same spot.

The biggest change to this crossroads, of course, is the pedestrianisation which has made the pubs, restaurants and retail stores far more accessible. The raised pavements and kerbs in the old picture became redundant, of course, and hence are missing in the new photograph.

The aforementioned *Marsden Grotto Inn* is filled with mystery, and sits on top of a network of interconnecting caves and tunnels which have never been fully explored. The oldest picture shows The Grotto as it appeared in the nineteenth century, and the snap was taken from the top of Marsden Rock which rests in the tempestuous North Sea only yards away from the pub. The sea wall, which is now forms a solid barrier against flash tides, is still under construction.

In the second picture we see a close-up shot of the inn from the shore. In the centre lies the lift shaft which ascends over one hundred feet to the cliff top above. To the right can be seen the steps – originally blasted into the cliff face by a former resident of the bay – which are available for more energetic types who scorn the use of the elevator.

The second floor of the building is a restaurant which has a reputation for good quality fayre, particularly its fish dishes.

The crossroads of Mile End Road (behind), King Street (right facing), Ocean Road (left facing) and Fowler Street (ahead) as workers were laying tram tracks for a new public transport network in the town. The trams were stored in a depot in Dean Road and provided a much-enhanced method of getting from A to B for commuters.

Just to the right of centre one can see the building that is now Barclays Bank, and in the distance, behind it, the corner of Keppel Street where Riddicks the shoe shop can now be found.

In the newer photograph the tram lines have all disappeared and been replaced with a pedestrianised plaza. Riddicks can be seen in the new photograph to the lower right of centre with its familiar green and cream paintwork.

Several managers and workers pose for the camera in the (then) new bus depot owned by the South Shields Corporation. In the background are several smartly-painted tram cars, whilst in the foreground are a number of pits used for maintenance of the carriages.

Above the workshop one can see a lattice of interconnecting steel girders which support the roof.

Today the depot is in the possession of the Stagecoach company which manages much of the local transport in the town. In the newer photograph is manager Steve Callaghan, who kindly gave the author and his wife a guided tour of the depot. The new photograph was taken from the same place as the first, and it can be seen that the original roof is still intact although the maintenance pits are now located elsewhere.

Steve can be seen standing in front of one of the large Stagecoach fleet buses that are a constant feature of life in South Shields today.

Ivor Mancey

Workers gather outside of the newly-constructed Tyne Dock railway station, which was a superbly-designed complex of buildings designed to enhance the rail network. At dawn special trains were laid on to take butchers to Newcastle upon Tyne where they would work in the markets.

Tyne Dock railway station is no longer with us, and has been replaced by a radically different Metro station (second picture). Today, Metro trains run up and down the line every few minutes, allowing passengers to travel all across Tyne & Wear incredibly quickly.

The Victorian architectural solidity of the old stations may be missing, but the Metro system is probably the best in Europe. The trains run on time and the carriages are almost always impeccably clean and in good repair. The futuristic design of the Metro stations would have probably shocked rail users of bygone times, but they'd surely have been impressed by both the technology and efficiency of our new network.

The old Brandling Junction railway station, named after the railway magnate Robert William Brandling, as sketched in the mid nineteenth century. The building was basic and provided only the barest of facilities for travellers. The original wooden structure was eventually replaced by brick.

In contrast, the second picture shows the entrance to South Shields Metro Station as viewed from the platform above King Street. Two flights of stairs are available for commuters wishing to ascend to the platform, plus a lift. Tickets are issued automatically from machines and an intercom device allows travellers to ask directions or details about services.

In stark contrast to the modern-looking station, its nice to see the presence of an old fashioned "fruit and veg" stall underneath the bridge where commuters can stock up on their "five a day" before going home to prepare dinner.

They certainly knew how to put on a show in those days. In the older picture, everyone who was anyone turned out for the official launch of the Electric Tram Service. The photograph was taken in South Eldon Street outside of the Freemasons Hall. The tram itself was destined for Boldon Lane, which by then was becoming popular with housewives as a good shopping area – particularly if you were on a tight budget.

To the right of the photo one can see the staff of the Fenwicks Dye Works & Laundry looking on excitedly from an upper window. Below is the shop owned by the Lawson family, well-respected purveyors (and repairers) of all manner of musical instruments.

In the second photograph we see a stark contrast. The ornate design of the tram has been replaced with the sleek, aerodynamic lines of the Metro train. However, there has been talk recently of re-introducing the tram system into South Shields – something that has been achieved successfully in other parts of the country.

The old coach in the first picture could hardly be called poster-fodder for public transport. It looks incredibly rickety and is topped with a bag which stored gas – fuel for buses in a time when petrol was in short supply. There isn't exactly a huge queue waiting to clamber on board, and by the look of the bus in question I'm not surprised.

Although it is sad that Souter no longer performs the purpose for which it was intended, South Tynesiders take comfort in the fact that it is still "open for business" and allows us to take a fascinating peek into its past.

How times change, though. The second picture shows the Stagecoach Number 8 service pulling up at the stop in Fowler Street as passengers prepare to embark for their journey to Horsley Hill or Marsden.

Fare prices have gone up, of course, but at this time of writing just £3.20 will get you an all-day ticket which will take you pretty much anywhere in the vicinity you could want to go.

South Tyneside Libraries

On June 11, 1832, two Jarrow pitmen, William Jobling and Ralph Armstrong, had been drinking in a pub in the centre of South Shields. As they made their way home the men bumped into an elderly magistrate called Nicholas Fairles and accosted him for money, presumably so they could continue their revelries. Fairles refused, and was promptly attacked by Armstrong who beat him severely with a stave and a large stone. The magistrate later died of his injuries. Armstrong fled the scene, but Jobling was arrested, tried and hung from a gibbet.

The first picture shows the house of Nicholas Fairles, which stood on the Lawe Top. The second shows Fairles Street, which was built later and named after the victim.

Argument still rages today about whether Jobling should have been hung. Some see him as an innocent victim of his friend's stupidity, whilst others feel that the sentence handed down was just. Personally I count myself among the latter party. The real victim was an elderly magistrate who was simply going about his business. Jobling may not have actually murdered Fairles, but he left the injured man alone to die.

A fascinating glimpse of Walter Scott's grocery store, which sold Sunlight soap, Fry's chocolate, Nestlés milk – and just about anything else your heart desired. A group of children stand in a huddle across the road, perhaps counting their pennies to see what treats they could afford. Behind them stands an ornate water fountain – another feature of life back then that is no longer with us.

General dealers are still found in profusion throughout South Shields, although specialisation is now the name of the game. The second photograph, taken in Dean Road in the late 1990s, illustrates the contrast well. To the left is LeeAnne's clothing store and O'Callaghan's the florist, whilst to the right sits a Co-operative Society "8 'til Late" store. The first two cater for specific markets, whilst the latter sold (and still sells) all the provisions available at Walter Scott's old shop and more.

The first picture shows Burrow Street and Fowler Street as they looked back in 1857. Giving due consideration to the fact that the image is a two-tone line drawing, the scene is still stark and unforgiving, Rows of tenement buildings, many in a poor state of repair, provided the barest of amenities for residents.

The second photograph shows Fowler Street as it is today; clean, well illuminated and a pleasant place to visit. No longer do we see tumbledown shops and corner-end off-licenses, but instead well-kept stores and neatly ashphalted roads.

In the second picture, workers wait for the regular bus services to take them home, whereas in 1857 there was no such luxury; one had to travel by "Shankses Ponies" – that is, on foot.

The first picture shows an old dwelling in Derby Terrace before it was demolished. The house has been turned into a "letter"; that is, an ale house registered with the local council but one which may not have had a proper name. Outside, a gas lamp provides illumination for passers-by, and a painted advertisement on the gable end speaks of the alcoholic beverages one may find inside.

The second picture shows Derby Terrace today. Old dwellings have been restored to something akin to their former glory, with the modern addition of UPVC doors and windows, whilst in the background sits a mixture of private dwellings and well-kept council housing stock.

One interesting feature of the new picture is the presence of a "speed bump"; a raised platform of ashphalt which forces vehicle drivers to moderate their speed – something that would have been totally unnecessary in the days of horse and trap.

Also available from Amberley Publishing

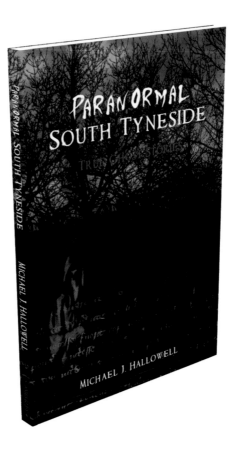

Paranormal South Tyneside
Michael J. Hallowell

Price: £12.99
ISBN: 978-1-84868-730-1

Available from all good bookshops or order direct from
our website www.amberley-books.com